72 Hours in Reykjavik

A smart swift guide to delicious food, great rooms and what to do in Reykjavik, Iceland.

TRIP PLANNER GUIDES

TABLE OF CONTENTS

Before You Get Started...   6

1   Welcome to Reykjavik   9

2   Reykjavik Districts   19

3   Day One in Reykjavik   26

4   Day Two in Reykjavik   39

5   Reykjavik Nightlife   44

6   Reykjavik Day Three   50

7   Reykjavik's Local Cuisine   60

8   Dining in Reykjavik   65

9   Reykjavik Accommodation   74

10 Reykjavik Travel Essentials   80

11 Additional Reykjavik Attractions   84

12 Icelandic Language Essentials   87

    Conclusion   98

BEFORE YOU GET STARTED

We've put together a quick set of tips for maximizing the information provided in this guide.

Insider tips: Found in italics throughout the guide, these are golden nuggets of information picked up during our travels. Use these handy tips to save money, skip the queues and uncover hidden gems.

Maps: This guide connects you to the most up-to-date city and transport maps. Step-by-step instructions are included on how to access. We highly recommend reviewing these maps PRIOR to departing on your trip.

Itineraries: While we have enclosed memorable itineraries for your use, we understand that sometimes you just want to venture out on your own. That is why all major attractions, hotels, restaurants and entertainment venues are tagged with the neighborhood that houses them. In doing so, you'll know what's nearby when planning your adventures.

Budget: Prices at time of publication are provided for all major attractions and a pricing scale is provided for all hotels, restaurants and entertainment.

Websites: To ensure you have the most up-to-date information prior to departure we have included links to venue websites for your convenience. Simply enter the url into your favorite browser to load the webpage.

1 WELCOME TO REYKJAVIK

As the northernmost capital of the world, Reykjavik provides a beautiful backdrop of awe-inspiring snow-topped mountains, volcanoes, and breathtaking ocean scenes. It has often been described as a true "winter wonderland" but it is more than this by far.

Reykjavik combines an intriguing mix of metropolitan energy and small town appeal, making it a city that truly has something for everyone. It has become an increasingly popular tourist destination and in this guide, we'll show you how to get the best out of this dynamic city.

While many places have been described as "colorful," one look around will tell you that Reykjavik truly is. Just look down any street, and you will be met with a view of vibrantly colored rooftops that double as navigation points to help you identify different areas of the city.

Although Reykjavik is a small city in comparison with other European destinations – Reykjavik only has a population of just over 200,000 people – this has the benefit of making the city's attractions accessible to visitors at all times of the year. This convenience, at least in part, lends to the city's cosmopolitan vibe placing it on a par with the best tourist destinations on the continent.

Cultural Interest

Reykjavik is the epicenter of Iceland's urban life and culture. As a result, it boasts a wide range of venues and events that attract music lovers, art enthusiasts and history buffs alike. Despite its diminutive size, this city crams in concert venues, theaters, art galleries and a wide range of museums.

Those interested in art or Iceland's history for that matter, will want to take note of the Reykjavik Asmundarsafn Art Museum, National Gallery of Iceland, and the Reykjavik City Museum. Drama is on offer too, and if you enjoy the theatre or sampling traditional Icelandic music, it is well worth seeking out tickets for Vesturport, Reykjavik City Theatre, and the National Theatre of Iceland.

Insider tip: Harpa Concert Hall alternates classic music concerts and other shows such as "How to become Icelandic in 60 minutes". Reykjavík gets most alive when special events are going on. The Secret Solstice Festival in June and Iceland

Airwaves in November are probably the most exciting, but New Year's Eve fireworks and atmosphere are simply unforgettable.

Music & Nightlife

If culture isn't your thing, don't be put off from visiting. Reykjavik has more to offer than Viking legends and picturesque views. The music scene here offers the kind of energetic nightlife that would rival that of any European capital. The streets of the city are dotted with pubs and top-shelf bars, making it a great place to drink, chat with friendly locals and relax. The focal point of the social scene is **Laugavegur**, a street where the nightlife of Reykjavik converges.

Insider tip: With concerts, shows, events and more there is no way of getting bored in the Icelandic Capital. Dozens of cafés and pubs offer live music every weekend and several of them do during the week as well (check the free paper Grapevine out to know what and where).

http://grapevine.is/

Yet, for all its energy, Reykjavik has a surprisingly laid-back ambiance that cannot be experienced anywhere else in the world. If you are looking for a great place to chill out and relax, a visit to Reykjavik will definitely fit the bill.

History

Reykjavik was inhabited by Icelanders for nearly a thousand years before it was developed into a town in the early 18th century. Legend has it that Ingólfur Arnarson, a Norwegian whose first name meant "royal wolf", first settled here in 874 AD. When his ship neared the island, he threw his high-seat pillars –wooden poles that were placed on either side of the head of the household's chair to indicate his status – overboard, vowing to build a settlement wherever they came ashore. True to his word he did so, and thus Reykjavik was founded. The name of the city comes from the hot springs in this area, which inspired the name Arnarson's settlement, "Smoky bay" or Reykjavik.

However, it wasn't until the 18th century, that the pastoral land of the area was developed into a town. In 1752, Frederik V, the King of Denmark, gave the estate of Reykjavik to Innréttingarnar. This industrial firm was expected to become a source of development in the country and a significant industrial exporter but it was unable to achieve its own high expectations. Despite this, the firm laid a good foundation for the city's industrial sector.

In 1801, Reykjavik was named the capital city of Iceland and in 1918, Iceland achieved its independence from Denmark.

Reykjavik was hit hard by the Great Depression but actually experienced a boom in its economy during the Second World War due to its occupation by British and US forces. The city experienced a massive growth in employment that led to the rapid modernization and expansion of its fishing fleet. In 1944, just before the end of the war, Iceland ceased to be a kingdom and became a republic.

A young city, Reykjavik doesn't possess the scenic old quarters and monumental buildings of other Nordic capitals. Instead, it is a modern city. Nevertheless it has the benefits of being "clean, green" and one of the safest cities in Europe.

Climate

Reykjavik has a subpolar oceanic climate, characterized by cool temperatures and often unpredictable weather. It isn't uncommon to experience clear skies one moment, followed by clouds and rain the next.

Useful Info at a Glance:

Mean Annual Temperature: 40 degrees Fahrenheit (4 degrees Celsius)

Average days of snow & rain: 148

Autumn: September & October - 44 degrees F (7 degrees C)

Cool and wet – prices & crowds drop

Special events (Reykjavik International Film Festival)

Winter: November - March - 35 degrees F (2 degrees C)

Cold & snow, but with lowest crowds & prices

Special events (Iceland Airwaves Music Festival, Reykjavik Fashion Festival)

Spring: <u>April & May</u> – 42 degrees F (6 degrees C)

Still cool but temps on the rise - prices & crowds lower than peak

Special events (Reykjavik Art Festival)

Summer: <u>June - August</u> - 55 degrees F (13 degrees C)

Warmest temps -crowds & prices are at their peak

Special events (Reykjavik Jazz Festival, Gay Pride, Reykjavik Marathon)

Insider tip: Summer is the peak travel season for visitors to Reykjavik. Outdoor activities and nature trips, such as horseback riding in the Snaefelsness glacier, scuba diving in Silfra, whale-watching in Faxaflói, and cave exploring in Gjabakkahellir will be most enjoyable in summer. However the "off season" is also attractive, offering reduced air fare and accommodation prices.

Language

The official language of Iceland is Icelandic, which is a dialect of "old Norse." A large number of

Reykjavik citizens also speak Danish, Norwegian, Swedish, and English.

Getting to Reykjavik

The best way to get to Reykjavik is to venture by plane and land at one of the city's two state-of-the-art airports, **Kelflavik International Airport** and **Reykjavik Airport**.

Kelflavik International Airport is the main international airport of the country, and serves as a hub to airlines like EasyJet, Delta Air Lines, German Wings, SAS, WOW air and Icelandair. Reykjavik Airport provides domestic flights to Vestmannaeyjar, Akureyri, and other destinations in Iceland.

Kelflavik International Airport

http://www.kefairport.is/english/

Reykjavik Airport

http://www.isavia.is/english/airports/reykjavik-international-airport/

Getting around Reykjavik

On Foot

Reykjavík is a small city and everything is within walking distance. Actually, walking is highly recommended as it gives you the chance to explore charming areas, in between the highlights. As you turn Reykjavik's many quiet corners, you will discover colorful houses and neat gardens, and resident wildlife. Wandering through the city gives you a chance to appreciate the first-rate pathway system and expansive green parks of **Klambratun** and the **Reykjavik Botanical Gardens**.

Biking

If you prefer to stay at ground level but move around a little faster, consider biking. While there aren't a lot of paths dedicated for bicycles here, it is legal to bike on sidewalks and streets. Just be prepared for a few hills and strong headwinds.

Car

Driving can be problematic for the tourist as most of the streets in the city are one-way, however including a GPS with your rental can alleviate this somewhat. A taxi cab is always an alternative option and all cabs are metered.

Bus

Strætó, Reykjavik's public bus system, is reliable, clean and fast. A single ride on this public transportation system normally costs 350 ISK. (The buses are unable to give change so you'll need to have the correct amount in Icelandic kronor.)

Insider tip: Stræto bus system offers frequent service: each part of the city has specific routes and the buses run in circles. From and to Keflavík

*International Airport, the **Flybus** is the only public transport available and you can choose the option that includes a stop at the Blue Lagoon on the way.*

Flybus

https://www.re.is/flybus/

If your travel extends beyond Reykjavik's center, consider purchasing a Reykjavik City card. This card grants free unlimited travel on buses within the Reykjavik Capital area as well as free access to several thermal pools, museums as well as discounts to several tours and entertainment. To purchase this pass, take a look at the listings posted on this website:

http://www.visitreykjavik.is/travel/reykjavik-city-card

It's possible to travel from Reykjavik and other cities in Iceland (which are invariably situated on the coasts as the interior of the country is filled with sand and lava flows, mountains and glaciers. Two bus operators provide bus transportation to and from cities within the country, "**Reykjavik Excursions**" and "**Sterna**."

Reykjavik

https://www.re.is/

Sterna

http://www.sternatravel.com/

2 REYKJAVIK DISTRICTS

Fully two-thirds of the population of Iceland lives in the city of Reykjavik and its surrounding suburbs or "metropolitan area" known as *Greater Reykjavik* or "the Capital Region." The rest of Iceland's residents live in coastal towns, as the interior of this island, called the "Highlands of Iceland" is uninhabitable.

Metropolitan Reykjavik

Reykjavik has a population of some 120,000 people, making it one of the smallest capital cities in the world.

The most important district is that of **Miðborg**, because it makes up the city center of Reykjavik. This district has six neighborhoods, and is also home to most of the city's tourist attractions, museums and nightlife. This will be the focal point of this guide, as most of your time will be spent here.

The Capital Region

Gardabaer

The district of Gardabaer, located south of Reykjavik, has about 20,000 residents, after its merger with the municipality of Alftanes in 2013. It is known for its historical and cultural heritage, as well as popular annual events such as its Jazz festival. There are also several nature reserves here. The spectacular Snæfells Glacier is also visible from many areas here. Gardabaer also is home to an Archeological Park and the Museum of Design & Applied Arts where tourists can experience Icelandic culture and history. The residence of the Governor of Reykjavik, Bessastaðir, is located here as well.

Hafnarfjörour

This port town of about 27,000 people is located about 10km south of Reykjavik and is the epitome of a vibrant Icelandic town. It is maybe best known for the annual Viking festival. Participants wear Viking clothing, participate in mock battles and display their skill in handicrafts. In truth, this place has everything; a piece of history, beautiful nature and, rumors are, they even have elves and trolls. You will see here a Bonsai garden, which is the northernmost in the world and truly a magical place.

Kjósarhreppur

The northernmost part of the Capitol Region, this is

also the smallest municipality, having only a little over 200 inhabitants.

Kópavogur

"Baby seal bay," about 12 minutes south of Reykjavik by car, is a mostly residential area of some 33,000 people, and the second largest city in Iceland after Reykjavik. There are a few venues here of interest to the tourist. Smaratorg Tower is one of them. It is one of the tallest buildings in Iceland, and at its base is a shopping mall. This neighborhood also has an art and history museum and thermal pools which are great for relaxing. Another visual highlight is the modern architecture you will find here; pay attention to the churches and the concert hall.

Mosfellsbaer

This neighborhood, about 7 miles east of Reykjavik, is nestled within mountains and is best known for its many recreational possibilities. People come here for golfing, hiking and cycling, climbing, horse riding, bird watching and more. Mt. Esja and Snæfellsjökul glacier, as well as Reykjavik itself, are visible when there's good weather. There are also excellent sport facilities which will enable you to fully enjoy your stay here.

Seltjarnarnes

This township, with about 4,000 inhabitants, is west of Reykjavik and is known for its beautiful coastal scenery and wealth of birdlife. Over 106 species of birds visit here over the course of a year. Seltjarnarnes is essentially a residential area, but the island of Grotta is a popular recreational area for both locals and tourists. Access is restricted here during nesting season in the month of June.

The city of Reykjavik itself has a population of about 120,000 people. If the Capital Region is included it has over 200,000 people. To this end, Reykjavik is more of big-town in comparison to most European cities and it is not overly difficult to find your way around as a visitor.

Yet heading off into a far corner of the city and getting hopelessly lost at the end of your day is never much fun. So, to this end, we recommend you always carry all the details of your place of accommodation (name address & phone number), as well as detailed maps of the areas you wish to explore.

Useful Maps & General Info

Maps are an invaluable asset for any curious traveler, especially one who wishes to get a little off the beaten path. There are a few elementary factors, however, which you should keep in mind when scouring the net or the book-shop for great maps of Reykjavik.

-They must be in both English AND Icelandic. Do not assume all locals will be able to read English and thus, be of any help to you.

-They must be recent. The names of streets and entire suburbs can change, and restaurants and cafés can move. Remember, outdated maps are as useful as non-existent ones.

-Whatever you do, locate, download, print and buy maps BEFORE you travel. The last thing you want to do is waste precious holiday time by looking for a printer or book stores when already in Reykjavik.

Here are some online maps, current at time of writing, which should help you make heads and tails of this wondrous city.

General City Map

The best overview maps online are courtesy of Michelin Maps. Go online here:

http://www.viamichelin.com/web/Maps/Map-Iceland

and have a look at the detailed map of Reykjavik. Click on the links up top to denote your desired attractions (hotels, restaurants, tourist attractions and even parking stations. You can calculate driving times and routes between two points, and even click on the weather icon to see the current weather conditions. Once you've zoomed in on your particular area of choice, simply click on the 'share' button, and proceed to 'print'.

Free Walking Tour of Reykjavik Meetup Location

Take this free, comprehensive walking tour and you'll stroll for 80-90 minutes exploring and enjoying the city of Reykjavik. You can see the meetup location map and view schedule information for 2015/2016 here: http://www.freewalkingtour.is/

GPS MY City App

This fantastic app can be downloaded, stored and used offline when in Reykjavik, requiring no internet coverage aboard. Click below to access 8 different walking tours with map.

http://tinyurl.com/mycityreykjavik

A light version can be downloaded free of charge while a full version is only $4.99 through the App Store.

Transportation Maps

For the Straeto bus network, click here:

http://tinyurl.com/straetobusmap

To print this map, simply right-mouse click on map and select 'print'

Official Tourism Website

Visit Reykjavik is the city's official tourism portal and packed with great info and up-to-date details on what's happening in and around the city, upcoming concerts, shows, events and more.

http://www.visitreykjavik.is/

Below is the address and contact details of the downtown Reykjavik Tourist Office:

Tourist Information Centre -Downtown Reykjavik

Adalstraeti 2

101 Reykjavik

Tel: +354 590 1550

3 DAY ONE IN REYKJAVIK

Despite its relatively small size, Reykjavik has plenty of attractions to keep visitors busy. For the first day of your trip to the capital of Iceland, you will take in the many sights of downtown Reykjavik, and when the night arrives we'll guide you to the perfect location to experience the Northern Lights.

A Walk through Reykjavik's Old Harbor

Name of Activity: Reykjavik Old Harbor

District: Miðborg (the city center)

Address: Ægisgarður 5

Phone #: +354 552 8211

Suggested arrival time: Any time of the morning or afternoon

Overview of Activity: Start the trip with a morning stroll to view the colorful fishing boats in the city's bustling harbor. Apart from watching the boats, the location of the harbor will also provide you with picturesque views of Esja peak (located about 10 km north of the city), and the gorgeous fjord to the southwest. The early morning is one of the best times to fully appreciate these sights.

The Old Harbor also houses several shops in which you can browse and this is also the location of the whale watching tour operators, and several restaurants. Further north is the **Viking Maritime Museum**.

Why you should go: The harbor puts on display the fascinating working life of Icelandic fishermen and the views are remarkable.

Directions: From the downtown Tourist Information Center, walk northwest 300 hundred meters on Vesturgata, and turn right on Norðurst. Once you cross Myrargata you will see all the sights of Old Harbor.

Website: http://www.oldharborreykjavik.com/

Grab a bite. If you haven't had breakfast, head off to the small 50's style café Grái Kötturin (the "Gray Cat," located at Hverfisgata 16a) It's open from 7:15 am to 3pm during the week, and from 8am to 3pm on the weekend.

Insider tip: Iceland could easily be the country with

the highest coffee consumption per capita in the world. Therefore, coffeehouses play a big role in Reykjavík. Downtown, the best ones are **Reykjavík Roasters** *(known for the best coffee in Iceland),* **Mokka** *(a sort of institution being the first café in the country),* **Kaffitár Bankastræti** *(which introduced fair trade coffee) and* **Babalú** *(an absolutely eccentric and lovely café). With more local atmosphere are* **Kaffihús Vesturbæjar** *in the west and* **Flóran Café** *in the Botanic Garden in the east. A refill of black coffee is usually included.*

Browse before you go:

Reykjavík Roasters

http://reykjavikroasters.is/

Mokka

http://www.mokka.is/Mokka/Mokka-Kaffi.html

Kaffitár Bankastræti

http://www.kaffitar.is/

Babalú

https://sites.google.com/a/babalu.is/babalu/

Kaffihús Vesturbæjar

http://kaffihusvesturbaejar.is/

Flóran Café

http://www.floran.is/floranenglish

A Visit to the Iconic Hallgrímskirkja Church

Name of Activity: Hallgrímskirkja Church

District: Miðborg (the city center)

Address: Hallgrímstorg 101

Operating hours: *Opening hours: 9 am to 9 pm during July and August, and 9am to 5pm from September to June.*

Cost: 800 ISK for tower admission for adults, 100 ISK for children.

Suggested arrival time & duration: Between 9 to 9:30 am, spending an hour to view.

Overview of Activity: For your next stop, make your way to the Hallgrímskirkja church, at Skólavörðustígur 101. Completed in 1986 after over 50 years of construction, this Lutheran cathedral, perched atop the hill called Skólavörðuholt in the center of the city, literally looks like a rocket ship. It is a beloved Icelandic structure that can be seen from a variety of vantage points in the city, making it an excellent navigational landmark.

To make your visit to this unforgettable cathedral, take an elevator ride to the top of the tower, where you'll have panoramic views of the city.

Why you should go: The design of this church is quite unique and the dizzying 360° view over Reykjavík is well worth it.

Directions: Hallgrímskirkja is visible from practically everywhere in the city. Simply keep heading toward its spire until you arrive! To its west is the Einar Jónsson Museum (on Eiriksgata) and Sculpture Garden (on Freyugata).

Website: http://www.hallgrimskirkja.is/

A Unique Collection of White-Marble Statues

Name of Activity: Einar Jónsson Museum

District: Miðborg (the city center)

Address: Eriksgata 3

Operating hours: *Tue- Sun 1 pm – 5 pm*

Phone #: +354 551 3797

Cost (in local currency): Museum entry is ISK 1000 for adults, under 18 free. Viewing the sculpture garden is free.

Suggested arrival time & duration: 1 pm to view the museum, any time to view the Sculpture Garden.

Overview of Activity: After you've taken your

photographs of the church, take a short walk to the Einar Jónsson Museum in Eiriksgata.

Einar Jónsson (1874-1954) trained as a sculptor at the Copenhagen Academy of Art in Denmark. When he returned to Iceland after living abroad for 20 years, the Icelandic parliament provided him with the funds to build a home and studio in Reykjavik. He designed the building himself and it is now a museum devoted to his life and works.

Einar Jónsson was a visionary, avant-garde thinker and sculptor and the art museum showcases a plethora of large art-deco sculptures. The real visual highlight of this art museum is in its garden, with stunning Gothic marble sculptures on display.

There is no need for you to go inside the museum (which costs ISK 1000), as you can see all the sculptors' masterpieces outside. The museum's hours vary depending on the season. The garden, however, is open to the public at any time of the day at no cost.

Why you should go: Apart from the well-known highlights, Reykjavík holds some treasures to discover and this is one. Despite its central location, entering the gates of the garden carries you to a silent world that is both charming and disquieting.

Directions: This museum sits across the street, to the west of the Hallgrímskirkja.

Website: http://www.lej.is/en/

Upon exiting the museum, follow Skólavörðustígur, the road in front of the dramatic statue of Leif Erikson (the first European in America) that leads from Hallgrímskirkja to Laugavegur, Reykjavik's main shopping street.

As you make your away down Laugavegur, you'll discover an assemblage of retail shops and smart boutiques touting fashion finds that range from vintage classics to concept-driven clothing.

*Insider tip: Another fascinating haunt is **Bókin**, located downtown within a stone's throw from Laugavegur at Klapparstígur 25-27. Open since 1964, this half brilliant and half chaotic bookstore is a heaven for booklovers, with thousands of books randomly placed everywhere, where you'll have the feeling that when looking for a book, you'll end up finding anything but that.*

http://www.bokin.is/

After shopping and wandering around the main retail street of Reykjavik, head down to Laekjargata, a street that leads from Laugavegur to the beautiful Tjörnin. This beautiful lake hosts scenic views and local wildlife.

Take your time and stroll around Tjörnin before entering the City Hall (Ráðhús) to view an astonishing 3D map that shows every single volcano, glacier, valley and village in the country.

Afterwards, enjoy a quick lunch before checking

out one of the two best museums (or both) out in the afternoon: the Viking-themed *Reykjavík 871 +/-2* and the historical *National Museum of Iceland*

If you are in the mood for seafood staples, try the delicious offerings at ***Fiskmarkadurinn*** (the Fish Market Restaurant) located just north of City Hall on Adalstraeti, 12. This restaurant boasts an innovative menu of fresh, top-quality seafood with Asian influences and flavors. Check out their Farmer's Market menu, comprised of Icelandic specialties such as halibut from Breiðafjörður, salmon from the Þjórsá and lobster from Höfn.

http://www.fiskmarkadurinn.is/

A Glimpse into the Viking Age

Name of Activity: Reykjavik 871 +/-2 (Settlement Exhibition)

District: Miðborg (the city center)

Address: Adalstraeti 16

Operating hours: *9am -8pm, daily*

Phone #: (+354) 411 6300

Cost (in local currency): 1,400 ISK Adults, children and 70+ free entry.

Suggested duration: 60-90 minutes

Overview of Activity: Learn about the first settlement of Iceland at this well preserved Settlement Exhibition. Here you will find remnants of a Viking longhouse from the 10th century in its original position, along with relics that date back to 871 A.D.

Why you should go: This is a unique opportunity to experience Viking life, straight from the pages of history.

Directions: 871/ +/-2 is steps away from *Fiskmarkadurinn* restaurant. However if you are coming from City Hall, follow Tjarnargata north to Kirkjustræti and make a right to arrive at the settlement exhibition.

Website: http://www.minjasafnreykjavikur.is/

Learn more about the City's History

Name of Activity: National Museum of Iceland

District: Miðborg (the city center)

Address: Suðurgötu 41

Operating hours: *10 am to 5 pm from May 1 to September 15, and 11 am to 5 pm from September 16 to April 30.*

Phone #: +354-530-2200

Cost (in local currency): 1500 ISK for adults. 750 ISK for students and senior citizens (67 years old and above). Guided tours are offered in English on Wednesdays, Saturdays and Sundays at 11am.

Suggested arrival time & duration: 10:45 to 11:30 am

Overview of Activity: The National Museum of Iceland is arguably the best and most important museum in the country. As the country's national museum, it presents an overview of the country's history (called Making of a Nation) from rustic artifacts to interactive videos. The museum has a dazzling array of exhibits that will give you insight into Iceland's history from the early Viking settlements to its impressive economic growth in the 20th century.

Why you should go: This is the easiest way to learn all about the country.

Directions: From City Hall, follow Tjarnargata south. Make a quick right onto Skothusvegur which will take you to the museum's street, Suðurgötu. Public buses no. 1, 3, 6, 11, 12 and 14 stop in front of or near the museum.

Website: http://www.thjodminjasafn.is/english

Get back to your accommodation, take a shower and get ready for the evening. **101** (this is how locals address to Reykjavík downtown, with its ZIP code) has plenty of restaurants, for any taste. Then, its time to see the Northern Lights.

The Northern Lights

The perfect way to end a day in Reykjavik is to witness an incredible natural phenomenon known as the Northern Lights. After enjoying your dinner, make your way to Grótta Lighthouse or "The Golf Course," which can offer fantastic views, away from the bright lights of the city. When the lights appear, they are often visible from eight in the evening up to three in the morning. To get here, hop on bus #11 and take it to Lindargotu Road. The lighthouse is a brief 5 minute walk from there.

Insider tip: The mesmerizing green lights of the Aurora Borealis can shine anytime over Reykjavík from September to April (with usual peaks in winter and sometimes early and late comers in August and May), but you need to be prepared to catch them.

Check the aurora forecast and with activity over 3/9 the odds are in your favour (for a stunning show, there's no need of very high activity). If this matches suitable weather conditions – which is to say fully or partly clear sky – just dress warm, set the camera, get away from light pollution, be patient and finally become enthralled with nature's fantastic display.

A good and near spot is the Grotta lighthouse at the far western end of the peninsula. It's a beautiful place to visit in general, however be sure to check the tide table below to ensure you aren't stranded during high-tide.

http://www.tide-forecast.com/locations/Reykjavik-Iceland/tides/latest

For more adventurous aurora hunts try the summit of Mount Esja, 10 km north of Reykjavík; for an amazing setting drive 45km to Þingvellir.

If you are unable to visit Reykjavik during these months, take in a movie instead.

Watch an Extraordinary Film about Iceland

Name of Activity: The Cinema/ the Cinema No. 2

District: Miðborg (the city center)

Address: Geirsgata 7b

Operating hours: *Noon to 8 pm*

Phone #: +354 898 6628

Cost (in local currency): Long shows, 1500 ISK, Short shows, 1000 ISK. Children 6 to 16 are half price, under 6 are free.

Overview of Activity: Tucked away in Reykjavik's Old Harbor, the Cinema (also called the Cinema No. 2) is a charismatic entertainment center.

Cinema No. 2 shows informative films like *Birth of an Island - The Making of Iceland* and *Chasing the Northern Lights*. These films give viewers an extensive insight on the country's most precious jewels and places.

The slate of films begins at noon with "Chasing the Northern Lights" and continues in rotation until 8 pm with the final showing of Birth of an Island. They also show films in German upon request.

Why you should go: The films provide a fascinating insight into the geology of Iceland.

Directions: Take a bus to the Harpa concert hall, and then walk west from there, enjoying a view of the harbor. It is about a 10 minute walk.

Website: http://www.thecinema.is/

4 DAY TWO IN REYKJAVIK

For the second day of your trip to Reykjavik, you will go on a day trip that will allow you to view the most spectacular natural wonders of Iceland. Make an early start for a countryside day trip. The Golden Circle includes three of the most astonishing natural wonders of the entire island: **Þingvellir National Park** -the location of the world's first parliament and the best spot on Earth to see the fissure created by two tectonic plates that are sliding apart, **Geysir** -the geothermal field with hot-water spouts after which this natural phenomena is named and **Gullfoss** -simply the most photogenic waterfall among the thousands you can find in the country.

Alternatively join a tour to Thrihnukagigur for the unique experience of descending into the magma chamber of a dormant volcano.

Insider tips: The most obvious day trip from Reykjavík is the Golden Circle, usually moderately crowded in winter but extraordinarily packed in summer. The warm season has very long days (never ending daylight for several weeks) and most of the visitors reach Þingvellir, Geysir and Gullfoss always around the same time, always in the same order. Exploit the light in early morning or late in the day (even at night) to have the 3 wonders all to yourself.

If driving, on your way back to Reykjavík, consider taking the road that leads to Selfoss for a stop in Kerið, an otherworldly explosion crater covered in moss that contains a dramatic green lake. Or, to avoid the masses, simply do the reverse Golden Circle, starting with Gullfoss; this trick often works to minimize crowds.

Why should I take the Golden Circle Route?

The Golden Circle Route is a day route that gives visitors the opportunity to experience the countryside charm of Iceland as well as take snapshots of its beautiful landscapes and natural wonders. It's a 190-mile round-trip journey, going in roughly a circle northeast to south and then back west and north to Reykjavik.

What are my options for this tourist route?

The Golden Circle route can be traveled by tour bus or a rented car.

While driving oneself can be a great and economical option for most Icelanders, another option for foreign travelers to avail themselves of the services of a tour company. Renting a car may offer flexibility, but taking a bus tour for some is more convenient.

There are several car rentals in Reykjavik, located mainly in the eastern suburbs and reachable by public bus (Stræto). It's important to note that the roads for these routes can be a bit slippery in any season, but especially during winter.

Tour operators

Several companies offer tours for this famous tourist route. The two most well known are Iceland Horizon and Iceland Excursions.

Iceland Horizon

A family-operated tour company, the Iceland Horizon is one of the most popular tour operators in the city of Reykjavik. They strive to keep your travel experiences fun, friendly and personal.

Address: Granaskjol 38, Reykjavik, Iceland

Contact number: +354 866 7237

Price per tourist: 9,900 ISK

Website: http://www.icelandhorizon.is/

Iceland Excursions

With over 25 years of experience in Icelandic tourism, Iceland Excursions is one of the most popular tour operators for the Golden Circle Route. A licensed travel agency, Iceland Excursions is truly a leading specialist in Iceland's tourism sector. Furthermore, it has a fleet of cutting-edge tour buses that come in array of sizes.

Address: Hafnarstraeti 20, 101 Reykjavik, Iceland

Contact number: +354 540 1313

Price per tourist: 9,375 ISK

Website: http://www.grayline.is/

Highlights of the Golden Circle Route

The Golden Circle Route tour will typically make its first stop at the historic site of Þingvellir National Park, located northeast of the city. A UNESCO World Heritage Site, Þingvellir National Park was the location of Iceland's parliament (Althing) – from 930 AD to 1798. The landscape here is also rather dramatic, as it is the place where the tectonic plates of North America and Europe meet, creating the Mid-Atlantic Ridge.

From Þingvellir National Park, the next destination is further east, the Geyser Geothermal area. Be sure to have your camera at the ready as the landscapes here are truly epic in scope.

The Geysir, also referred as "The Great Geysir" was the first geyser ever discovered. In fact, the Icelandic term for this natural phenomena has entered all languages.

Although the Great Geyser itself doesn't erupt frequently, Strokkur (the smaller geyser) gushes jets of water into the air every eight minutes or so. There are a few other small geysers to be seen here as well.

Some tours will stop at the Information Center here for lunch, while others will go on in a northeast direction to the Gullfoss.

Aptly named as the "Golden Falls," the Gullfoss is a striking two-tiered waterfall which is a staple in many Golden Circle Route tours. Visitors witness an endless flow of water crashing into a rift with a sound like thunder, and the mists rising can be seen for miles.

The Gullfoss is a popular luncheon spot as well. Tourists usually head to the Gullfoss café to savor delectable lunch meals and treats. The next stops on the tour come on the route south toward Kerið, and include Skalholt Church, Mt. Hengil Volcano, Langjkull Glacier and Hverageroi, before finally returning west to Reykjavik.

5 REYKJAVIK NIGHTLIFE

Reykjavik has a multitude of nightlife offerings, from live bands and disco clubs to cozy pubs and luxurious lounges. Wherever you go, you will find high-quality local beers and strong Icelandic schnapps.

The focal point of Reykjavik's nightlife is its main street, Laugavegur. Here, you can pick your poison from over fifty nightlife venues. But with so many options available, how can you pick the right place to go? Let us suggest a few.

Insider tip: The djammið is the most Icelandic way of enjoying a Friday or a Saturday night. It might sound complicated to find 10 pubs (or more) to visit during the same night, but by the time its over you'll regret not having more time (or energy) for the tens more you couldn't include in your pub crawl.

*Excellent venues to begin with are **Prikið** (cool little bar with great atmosphere), **Mikkeller & Friends*** *(where you'll find dozens of microbrewed beers to sample before choosing),* **Den Danske Kro** *(authentic Danish style) and* **Slippbarinn** *(for fancy drinks).*

Don't be shy! Join a few locals to go discover other prominent pubs and meet more newcomers as well. Keep in mind that March 1 is officially Beer Day!

Browse before you go:

Prikið

http://prikid.is/

Mikkeller & Friends

http://mikkeller.dk/mikkeller-friends-reykjavik/

Den Danske Kro

http://www.danski.is/

Slippbarinn

http://www.slippbarinn.is/en

Kaffibarinn: The Trendiest Night Spot in Town

This venue might be bit small for your taste, but Kaffibarinn is certainly the standard-bearer of Reykjavik's nightlife. As a matter of fact, many people even think that Kaffibarinn is the venue responsible for making the city's reputation as a party capital. Featuring a trendy bohemian vibe, the bar is truly a cozy gem with hyper-cool electronic music, beautiful people, delicious cocktails, frozen bottles of beer and stylish decorations. If you want to experience the essence of Icelandic nightlife, the Kaffibarinn is your best bet.

Additional information:

Opening hours: 4:30 pm to 1:00 am from Sunday to Thursday. 5:00 pm to 4:30 am on Fridays and Saturdays.

Address: Bergstadastraeti 1, Reykjavik, Iceland

Contact number: +354 551 1588

http://www.kaffibarinn.is/

District: Miðborg

Dillon Whiskey Bar: Fine Whiskeys with Classic Rock Music

Known as Iceland's largest whisky bar, Dillon Whiskey Bar has a seemingly endless selection of beers and of course, whiskies. The venue also plays cool classic rock tunes from some of the city's finest rock bands for guests to savor in its rustic ambiance.

Additional information

Opening hours: 2 pm to 1 am from Sunday to

Thursday. 2 pm to 3 am on Fridays and Saturdays.

Address: Laugarvegur 30, 101 Reykjavik, Iceland

Contact Number: +354 578 2411

http://dillon.is/

District: Miðborg

Lebowski Bar: A Cushy and Modish Themed Bar

Does the name ring a bell? This Icelandic bar is named after the famous 1998 comedy film *The Big Lebowski*. As you would expect, the bar has a cushy and stylish interior complete with bowling alley and Americana, and has been called the "coolest bar theme" in all of Iceland. Their beers, milkshakes and big juicy burgers are renowned.

Additional information

Opening hours: 11 am to 1 am from Sunday to Thursday. 11 am to 4 pm on Fridays and Saturdays.

Address: Laugarvegur 20a, 101 Reykjavik, Iceland

Contact number: +354 552 2300

http://www.lebowskibar.is/

District: Miðborg

English Pub: A Classy Bar with a twist

The English Pub is a classy and unique pub that serves more than 30 of the finest brands of whiskey, ale and beer to the thirsty party-holics of the city. It also features a game called 'wheel of fortune,' where a guest can win a meter of high-quality beer. The pub features troubadours and cover bands that play catchy tunes which appeal to all kinds of party goers.

Additional information

Opening hours: 12 pm to 1 am from Sunday to Thursday. 12 pm to 5 am on Fridays on Saturdays.

Address: Austerstraeti 12A, Reykjavik, Iceland

Contact number: +354 578 0400

http://www.enskibarinn.is/en/

District: Miðborg

Boston: A Relaxing Nightlife Offering

A breath of fresh air in the city's nightlife scene, Boston has a very laid-back vibe suitable for people who simply want to chill out and have good conversation. It has a stylish interior embellished with antique furniture, glass mosaics, and animal trophies. The soft lighting enhances the laid-back atmosphere as guests enjoy oldies and jazz music. On the second floor of the bar is a patio where guests can sit, drink and enjoy the views of the old city.

Additional information

Opening hours: 7 pm to 1 am on Sundays. 4 pm to 1 am from Monday to Thursday. 4 pm to 3 am on Fridays and Saturdays.

Address: Laugarvegur 28b, Reykjavik, Iceland

Contact number: +354 517 7816

FB: https://www.facebook.com/boston.reykjavik

District: Miðborg

Helpful tips

There is no cover charge for most clubs, bars and lounges in Reykjavik. However, if you're going to a venue that offers live music, expect to pay a bit to gain entry. The minimum drinking age is twenty years old -keep an ID handy.

While Reykjavik's nightlife buzzes every day of the week, on weekends the hours are extended, and it's the time when some of the best musicians in the city are featured at various venues.

6 REYKJAVIK DAY THREE

It's your third day in Reykjavik and with the key attractions out of the way, let's slow down the pace for today. An excellent way is to begin with a soak in the thermal waters of Laugardalslaug, 2 km east from the city center.

Insider tips: Swimming pools and hot pots are the most common gathering place for Icelanders, just like saunas are for Finnish or hammams for Turkish. The Blue Lagoon is unmissable but it's not where Icelanders usually go and it has a very touristy atmosphere. For a local feel visit try Laugardalslaug or Árbæjarlaug instead. Another option, for sunny Summer days, is the beach of Nauthólsvík, behind the University of Reykjavík, where the water of the Atlantic is artificially heated and the sand imported from Morocco.

Name of Activity: Laugardalslaug Thermal Pools

District: Laugardalur

Address: Sundlaugarvegur, 104 Reykjavik

Operating hours: *Opening hours: 6.30am-10pm Mon-Fri, 8am-10pm Sat & Sun*

Cost: Adults: 650 ISK, Kids: 140 ISK

Suggested duration: At least an hour

Overview of Activity: Well worth a visit, the thermal pools of Laugardalslaug are perfect for soaking weary muscles or simply unwinding during your travels. This "hot springs garden" has the largest outdoor thermal pool in the city which offers swimming in every season of the year. There's also a zoo botanical gardens, and hiking and biking trails nearby.

Why you should go: Skip the well-touristed Blue Lagoon and go where the Icelanders go to soak in the welcoming thermal pools and steam rooms.

Directions: The thermal pools are located just 2km west of the city center and serviced by bus routes 12 and 14.

Website: http://www.itr.is/

Alternatively, for many no trip to the city of Reykjavik is complete without a visit to Iceland's most famous man-made wonder, the Blue Lagoon geothermal spa.

The World-Famous Blue Lagoon

Name of Activity: The Blue Lagoon

District: Reykjanes Peninsula

Address: 240 Grindavík

Operating hours: *Daily 9am to 8 pm. For the current schedule including holidays click here*: *http://www.bluelagoon.com/plan-your-visit/opening-hours/*

Phone #: +354 420 8800

Reservation#: http://www.bluelagoon.com/blue-lagoon-spa/prices-and-packages/

Cost (in local currency): Standard ticket, 6,606 ISK. Comfort, 8,808, Premium, 11,010, Luxury, 24,220 ISK. Pre-booking is required.

Suggested arrival time & duration: Between 2 to 3pm

Overview of Activity: The Blue Lagoon allows you to relax in crystal blue water that is always 37-40°C (98-104°F). The Blue Lagoon is anywhere from 0.8-1.2 meters deep and is 1.6 meters deep at its deepest point.

The Standard ticket gives you entrance to the Blue Lagoon, the Comfort ticket includes a towel, a drink of your choice and a skin care trial pack, and the Premium ticket includes entrance to the Blue

Lagoon, use of bathrobe, towel and slippers, and a reserve table at their restaurant, LAVA. The luxury ticket also includes entry to the exclusive lounge.

Why you should go: The waters of the Blue Lagoon have health giving properties and gives you the full spa experience highlighted by the beautiful landscape.

Directions: If driving, take Route 41 which connects Reykjavik to Keflavik, and continue south on Route 34. After five miles, take a right onto Route 426. Then, just follow the signs. It's about 47 km from Reykjavik to the Blue Lagoon, or a 50 minute drive depending on traffic.

Bus -Head to Reykjavik's BSI terminal and board the bus for the Blue Lagoon. Scheduled depart times are listed here:

https://www.re.is/blue-lagoon-schedule

The transfer costs 3.600 ISK for adults, 1.800 ISK for ages 14-15yrs and children 0-13yrs are free.

Website: http://www.bluelagoon.com

A Green Retreat within the City

Name of Activity: The Botanic Gardens

District: Laugardalur

Address: Laugardalur, 104 Reykjavík

Operating hours: *Opening hours: 6.30am-10pm Mon-Thurs, Fri 6.30am-8pm, 9am-6pm Sat & Sun*

Cost: Entrance to the Botanic Garden is free.

Suggested duration: At least an hour

Overview of Activity: Reykjavik's Botanic Garden is a beautiful collection of over 5000 plant species, tranquil walking paths and you may find yourself making friends with a duck or two at the picturesque pond. While the Reykjavik is renowned for its natural wonders outside of the city, the Botanic Gardens provided a green retreat within the city for those short on time.

Why you should go: In addition to strolling through an extensive collection of subarctic plant species, the onsite Flóran Café is the perfect respite for lunch.

Directions: The Botanic Gardens are a short distance from the Laugardalslaug thermal pools and serviced by bus routes 2, 14, 15, 17 and 19.

Website: www.grasagardur.is

After returning from the thermal pools, why not spend the afternoon strolling along the northern coast of the city's beautiful Faxaflói Bay. We'll go from east to west, and the first stop is the shiny skeletal sculpture of a ship *Sólfar* - The Sun Voyager.

Name of Activity: Sólfar - The Sun Voyager

Address: Saebraut, Reykjavik

Opening hours: 24 hours

Cost: Free

Suggested duration: 20-30 minutes depending on the weather. For stunning photos return here during sunrise, or sunset.

Overview of Activity: Sólfar Sculpture or the Sun Voyager in Saebraut was created by sculptor Jón Gunnar Árnason in 1986 to celebrate the 200th anniversary of the city of Reykjavik. Crafted from aluminum, the sculpture is in the shape of a Viking long-boat.

Why you should go: Resting along the coastline, this well-crafted sculpture is an undisputed symbol of the Icelandic Capital.

Directions: Sólfar is located a short, walkable distance from downtown Reykjavik. From downtown, follow Lækjargata to reach the northern shore. Head east and you will find the silver sculpture positioned along the waterfront in Saebraut.

Website: http://sunvoyageris.com/

Next stop is Harpa, the glass concert hall and cultural center of Reykjavik.

Name of Activity: Harpa Concert Hall

Address: Austurbakka 2, 101 Reykjavík

Opening hours: *10am-6pm, daily.*

Cost: Guided tours of the building are available for 1.750 per ISK person. The tour lasts 45minutes and the seasonal timetable can be viewed here:

http://en.harpa.is/access/harpa-guided-tours

Concert Ticket Reservations: (+354) 528 5050

Suggested duration: 45 minutes to an hour

Overview of Activity: Harpa is Reykjavik's concert hall and conference center, located near the old harbor. Deigned be the Danish firm Henning Larsen Architects in partnership with Danish-Icelandic artist Olafur Eliasson, the building is comprised of metal framework covered with geometric glass panels. Even if you don't want to attend a show here, take an hour or so to wander through the building as it is worth your time.

Why you should go: This beautiful glass structure is an architectural wonder.

Directions: From Sólfar, take a brief walk west

along the coastline to reach Harpa.

Website: http://en.harpa.is/

*Insider's tip: On the hunt for a bargain? If you're here during the weekend, swing by the **Kolaportið Flea Market** as you walk towards the Old Harbour. Located at Tryggvagötu 19, you'll find new and used wares featuring everything from food and clothing to household good and antiques. You can even pick up shark meat if your first bit of Hákarl wasn't enough to tide you over.*

http://www.kolaportid.is/

After an afternoon along the shore, bring your third day to a close by learning more about Iceland's volcanoes at Volcano House.

Name of Activity: Volcano House

District: The Old Harbor

Address: Tryggvagata 11

Operating hours: Open every day from 10:00 am to 9:00pm every day including Easter. Shows start every hour on the hour.

Phone #: +354 555 1900

Cost (in local currency): 1990 ISK per adult, senior citizens and students are 1700 ISK. Children between 12-16yrs, 1000 ISK. Children under 12 are free.

Suggested duration: Around one hour for the documentaries.

Overview of Activity: The Volcano House cinema presents two documentaries, "The 1973 eruption on the Westman Islands," and "Eyjafjallajökull and Fimmvörðuháls eruptions of 2010." The two documentaries together last for one hour.

After viewing the documentaries, browse through their geology exhibit and then head to their boutique to purchase lava rocks, bottles of ash, pumice, or books and DVDs on volcanoes.

Why you should go: Iceland is a country of contrasts – of fire and ice. This is brought home to you as you view these two gripping documentaries.

Directions: Volcano House is located in the Old Harbor, in Reykjavik's City Centre. It is only a hundred meters west of the Main Tourist Office.

Website: http://www.volcanohouse.is/

End the day in the Old Harbour neighborhood, visiting the off the beaten track **Maritime Museum** or simply having dinner with lobster soup at **Sægreifinn** or a lamburger at **Hamborgarabúllan**

Sægreifinn

http://saegreifinn.is/

Hamborgarabúllan

http://www.bullan.is/

7 REYKJAVIK'S LOCAL CUISINE

Every country has famous dishes which are available nowhere else in the world, and some of which you may approach with caution.

There's the haggis of Scotland, for example, which consists of a sheep's heart, liver and lungs (otherwise known as "pluck") minced together with other ingredients such oatmeal and then encased in its stomach. Icelanders also have culinary delicacies that foreigners may tempted to try *very carefully*. Here is a list of common, and not so common dishes to try during your travels in Reykjavik.

Meat preservation

Throughout history in most parts of the world, meat was preserved by curing it with salt. However in Iceland, due to a lack of salt, inhabitants in the 14th century began to cure their meat in fermented whey or brine. To this day that is how most meat is preserved and it is what gives Icelandic cuisine its distinctive flavors. Most of Iceland's traditional dishes are meat-based with vegetables as the side dish. The meat can be lamb, mutton or horsemeat.

Lamb

One of the reasons why Icelandic lamb tastes so good is that the animals are not subjected to antibiotics or hormones. Additionally, there is little need for pesticides or herbicides here, and Iceland has strict regulations governing agriculture.

As a result, the animals roam free and eat the food they were meant to eat. They are only rounded up once a year, therefore fresh lamb is available from September through December only.

Hangikjöt

Hangikjöt ("hung meat") is a Christmas dish that consists of smoked lamb, mutton or horsemeat. The flavors are like nothing you have tasted elsewhere. The meat is boiled, then sliced thinly and served either hot or cold. Traditionally, the side dishes are green peas and potatoes in a white sauce.

Svið

Svið is quite a popular dish in Iceland. It is a sheep's head that has been cut in half, and then boiled. In case you are wondering, the brains have been removed. The dish is served with vegetables such as mashed potatoes, carrots, or turnips. Most of the meat is found in the cheek, and the eyeballs are considered a delicacy.

Seafood

Hákarl

Probably the most unusual seafood dish offered on the menu of Icelandic restaurants is Hákarl, which is the flesh of Greenland shark that has been buried in the ground and fermented for six months in order to remove the toxins in the meat. Considered a delicacy, it is best to sample this pungent meat in small quantities.

Insider tip: This dish, though served in small portions is not for the faint of heart. The smell may get to you long before the taste. Should you decide embark on this culinary adventure, do like the locals and chase with a shot of brennivín.

Harðfiskur

A favorite snack consumed by people of all ages is harðfiskur. This is fish (usually cod, haddock or seawolf) that has been filleted and then hung on a drying rack to dry in the wind.

If you go to a movie anywhere else you probably eat popcorn. In Iceland, you'll probably eat harðfiskur – tearing off a piece, dipping it in salted butter, and then letting it melt in your mouth.

Poultry

Norse settlers brought chickens with them to Iceland in the ninth century, and this hearty breed survives to the present day. However, other poultry can be found on the menu, for example puffin. Puffin meat is usually smoked and is considered a delicacy.

Dessert

Skyr

Skyr is an incredibly popular desert in Iceland and is available everywhere. It is similar to yogurt. It can be eaten on its own or topped with berries.

Alcohol

Many Icelanders celebrate March 1 as "beer day." That's the day that the prohibition on "strong beer," which began in 1915, was lifted...in 1989! Bars stay open longer and many people go on a "rúntur" (bar crawl) to enjoy the many Icelandic beers.

There's also brennivín, a type of schnapps made of potatoes and caraway seeds. This drink also carries the famous nickname *svarti dauði* or "black death."

To ensure that you can sample all of Iceland's most popular dishes, consider taking part in the Reykjavik Food Tour. Your guide will lead you through restaurants and gourmet shops in the city that will provide you samples of different local specialties.

For those who would like to learn how to cook fish and lamb the Icelandic way, attend a cooking class offered by Salt Eldhus Cooking School. You will get to have fun, cook under close supervision of their chefs, and taste the dishes that you have created.

Reykjavik Food Tour

http://reykjavikfoodtour.com/

Salt Eldhus Cooking School
http://www.visitreykjavik.is/salt-eldhus

8 DINING IN REYKJAVIK

From traditional Nordic dishes to contemporary international meals, Reykjavik possesses an eclectic selection of culinary offerings that will gratify your taste buds. What's more, the city is abundant in sources for fresh meat and seafood, and foodies will certainly enjoy sampling the culinary delights of this city.

Insider tips: Reykjavík offers a wide range of excellent dining options, from brunch places like **The Coocoo's nest** *and* **Public House** *to chic bistros like* **Snaps** *and* **KOL**. *There's also the cosy atmosphere of* **Forettabarinn** *and* **Fiskmarkaðurinn** *and the unique settings of* **Apótek** *and* **Perlan**.

You'll also find the international cuisine of **Tapas Barinn** *and* **Osushi the train** *to high quality fast food like* **Sægreifinn** *and* **Hamborgarabúllan**.

Without forgetting street food: **Mandi's kebabs**,

Bæjarins' hot dogs *and* ***Lobster Hut's subs*** *are probably the best picks.*

Key:

Budget: 2,000 ISK

Mid-range: 4,000 – 8,000 ISK

Deluxe: 10,000 ISK upward

Budget options

C is for Cookie Restaurant

Known for its cookies, of course, this coffee shop also offers cheesecakes that are to die for. It possesses a colorful bohemian vibe, friendly staff and above all, affordable tasty treats. Whether you are sipping from a cup of coffee, cappuccino or tea, this café is a great place to relax as well as enjoy a snack during a cold windy day in the city.

Address: Tysgata 8, Reykjavik, Iceland

Contact number: +353 578 5914

FB: https://www.facebook.com/cookie.reykjavik

District: Miðborg

Nudluskalin Restaurant

Despite its small space, the Nudluskalin Restaurant is considered by many foodies as one the best places to dine in Reykjavik. Not only does it have a cozy and romantic ambiance, but it also serves a variety of hearty noodle meals, made from fresh produce.

Skolavordustig 8, Reykjavik 101, Iceland

+354 562 0202

http://www.nudluskalin.com/

District: Miðborg

Ida Zimsen Restaurant

Book lovers must be sure to check out the Ida Zimsen Restaurant in Vesturgata. Located right in the heart of the city, this restaurant is famous for it's chilled out atmosphere, sumptuous cakes, high-quality coffee, and of course, books.

Vesturgata 2a, 101 Reykjavik, Iceland

+354 551 5004

FB: https://www.facebook.com/IdaZimsen

District: Miðborg

Mid-range

Glo Restaurant

For a healthy and filling vegetarian meal in Reykjavik, head down to the award-winning Glo Restaurant. From veggie wraps to awesome vegan potatoes and pumpkin soup, this restaurant has a load of culinary offerings that will please health-conscious eaters.

Address: Engjateigur 19, Laugavegur 20b, Reykjavik, Iceland

Contact number: +354 553 1111

http://www.glo.is/

District: Miðborg

Svarta Kaffi Restaurant

Looking for delicious homemade soups with fresh bread? The Svarta Kaffi Restaurant is your best bet. In addition to its amazing soups and freshly baked bread, it has a terrific setting and is quite affordable compared to other restaurants in the city.

Address: Laugavegi 54, 101, Reykjavik, Iceland

Contact number: +354 551 2999

FB: https://www.facebook.com/svartakaffid#_=_

District: Miðborg

Sjavargrillid Restaurant

Sjavargrillid Restaurant, or the "Seafood Grill," is hands down one of the finest seafood restaurants in the country. Spearheaded by Chef Gustav Gunnlaugsson, this seafood restaurant has a broad menu of seafood staples and Icelandic treats. On top of that, the restaurant has a cozy and warm lodge feel, giving you an unforgettable dining experience.

Address: Skolavordustigur 14, Reykjavik, Iceland

Contact number: +354 571 1100

http://www.sjavargrillid.com/

District: Miðborg

Deluxe

Fridrik V Restaurant

The award-winning Fridrik V Restaurant is arguably Iceland's finest and most beloved Scandinavian restaurant. The Fridrik V is small and cozy and it's essential that you call ahead for reservations. They offer three- and five-course dinners with wine pairings. .

Address: Laugavegur 60, Reykjavik 101, Iceland

Contact number: +354 461 5775

http://www.fridrikv.is/en/

District: Miðborg

Kol Restaurant

From service and food quality to interior design, nearly every aspect of the Kol Restaurant is perfect. It's another small restaurant with an intimate atmosphere so be sure to make reservations. They offer Icelandic and international dishes.

Skolavordustigur 40, Reykjavik 101, Iceland

Contact number: +354 517 7474

http://kolrestaurant.is/en/

District: Miðborg

Dill Restaurant

Upon arrival, the restaurant's staff will present you

with a chilled, complementary bottle of champagne. Afterwards, you will pick your meals from a wide selection of Scandinavian, Danish and Swedish dishes. Besides its exceptional culinary offerings, the restaurant boasts a dramatic and comfortable ambiance as well. Dill is open for dinner only, from Wednesdays through Saturdays.

Hverfisgata, Reykjavik 101, Iceland

Contact number: +354 552 1522

http://dillrestaurant.is/en

District: Miðborg

Additional Options:

The Coocoo's nest

https://www.facebook.com/cafecoocoos

Public House

http://www.publichouse.is/

Snaps

http://www2.snaps.is/?lang=en

KOL.

http://kolrestaurant.is/

Forettabarinn

http://forrettabarinn.is/

Fiskmarkaðurinn

http://fiskmarkadurinn.is/

Apótek

http://apotekrestaurant.is/?lang=en

Perlan

http://www.perlan.is/?lang=en

Tapas Barinn

http://www.tapas.is/is/

Osushi the train

http://www.osushi.is/

Sægreifinn

http://saegreifinn.is/

Hamborgarabúllan.

http://www.bullan.is/

Mandi's kebabs

http://mandi.is/

Bæjarins' hot dogs

http://www.bbp.is/

Lobster Hut's subs

https://www.facebook.com/Lobster-Hut-1411706319113011/

9 REYKJAVIK ACCOMMODATION

Reykjavik features accommodation options that range from world-class resorts and luxurious boutique hotels to cheap hostels and campsites.

Key:

(Note that rates per night vary by season)

Budget: 10,000 ISK

Mid-range: 13,315 – 26,631 ISK

Deluxe: 33,288 ISK upward

Budget Options

Minna-Mosfell Guesthouse

With its tranquil and relaxing feel, the Minna-Mosfell Guesthouse will enable you to relax after a busy day in the city. Enjoy being treated to jam, freshly made pancakes and bread for breakfast daily. The guesthouse is located 20 minutes from downtown Reykjavik.

Address: Mosfellsbaer, Reykjavik 271, Iceland

+354 669 0366

http://www.minnamosfell.net/

District: Mosfellsdalur Valley

Reykjavik Hostel Village

With its convenient location, right downtown, and affordable rates, the Reykjavik Hostel Village has become a favorite retreat among budget-conscious travelers and backpackers. In addition to its great location, the hostel also has excellent facilities and amenities, including free parking and Wi-Fi.

Address: Flókagata 1, 105 Reykjavik, Iceland

+ 354 552 1155

http://www.hostelvillage.is/

District: Miðborg

Reykjavik Backpackers Hostel

The Reykjavik Backpackers Hostel is, as the name implies, designed for backpackers and caters to those looking for a way cut down their expenses during their trip to Reykjavik. Nestled right at the heart of the city, the hostel also has a good location with the city's best attractions just a few yards away.

Address: Laugavegur 28, 101 Reykjavik, Iceland

http://www.reykjavikbackpackers.is/

District: Miðborg

Kex Hostel

Kex Hostel also caters to young travelers, especially backpackers. It is famous for its hip and trendy vibes, and offers everything a traveler would need. They offer a restaurant, bar, and heated outdoor patio, as well as guest kitchens, a laundry room and even a gym.

Address: Skulagata 28, Reykjavik 101, Iceland

+354 561 6060

http://www.kexhostel.is/

District: Miðborg

Mid-range

CenterHotel Plaza

CenterHotel Plaza has 200 rooms and meeting and conference facilities. Each room has free internet, a flat screen TV, and a mini bar.

Address: Adalstraeti 4, 101 Reykjavik, Iceland

http://www.centerhotels.com/our-hotels/hotel-plaza

District: Miðborg

Fosshotel Lind

The Fosshotel Lind is located in downtown Reykjavik and gives its guests easy access to the city's most celebrated landmarks and attractions, including the striking Hallgrimskirkja Church, Harpa Concert Hall, Sun Voyager sculpture and many more. There are 70 well-designed suites with all the amenities that travelers have come to expect.

Address: Raudararstigur 18, Reykjavik 101, Iceland

http://www.fosshotel.is/

District: Miðborg

Deluxe accommodations

Black Pearl

Ever since it opened in 2013, Black Pearl apartments and hotel has become noted the true epitome of class and sophistication when it comes to five-star lodgings. Black Pearl has an opulent and idyllic feel that will give you a slice of heaven on earth. The hotel features a penthouse as well as deluxe and standard suites.

Address: Tryggvagata, 18/18c, Reykjavik 101, Iceland

http://www.blackpearlreykjavik.com/

District: Miðborg

Hotel Borg

Overlooking iconic Asuturvollur Square in the heart of Reykjavik, Hotel Borg is an elegant and sleek Art Deco hotel. As an upscale hotel, Hotel Borg offers comfortable premium beds and spacious room embellished with stylish furniture and hardwood floors.

Address: Pósthússtræti 11, 101 Reykjavík

http://en.hotelborg.is/

District: Miðborg

Reykjavik Residence

The Reykjavik Residences is a world-class hotel with stylish accommodations and luxurious amenities such as free Wi-Fi, iPod docking stations and modern kitchen facilities. Moreover, it is located only a few yards from the shopping center of Laugavegur.

Address: Hverfisgata 21, 101 Reykjavík

http://www.rrhotel.is/

District: Miðborg

10 REYKJAVIK TRAVEL ESSENTIALS

Here is some practical information that you can use when traveling to Reykjavik:

Currency

Currency used in Reykjavik is the Icelandic Krone (ISK). It is pronounced *krona*, which means crown. The Icelandic Krone is the only currency that you can use, since Iceland is not part of the European Union and does not use Euro. (Having said that, you will sometimes see prices quoted in Euros if you visit hotel or tourism sites – just bear in mind that you will actually have to pay in ISK.)

You can get cash at banks and exchange offices in the city and at the airport and there are ATM machines everywhere. You can use cash in Reykjavik for any purchases, but the locals mostly use credit cards. Major credit cards are typically accepted at restaurants and lodgings throughout Reykjavik.

Phone Calls

If someone from Europe tries to reach you at a land line in Reykjavik, they will need to enter the country code which is (00)354 and then enter a seven digit number. The first of the 7 digits will be 5 for calling Reykjavik.

If someone tries to call you from the USA or Canada, the only difference is that they will have to enter a different exit code before dialing your number (for the USA is 011). The process is the same when it comes to dialing mobile phones, however it is important to note that mobile numbers can have 7 or 9 digits.

To call European countries from Iceland enter 00 followed by the phone number. If you call the USA dial 001 and then the appropriate phone number.

As with the rest of the world, it is very difficult to find payphones in Reykjavik, so if you don't have a mobile phone with international access you will have to call from your hotel's landline.

Standard Mealtimes

Standard times that meals are served can vary. If you are staying in a hotel, you can expect breakfast buffets to be served 5.00am-10.00am. Lunch is often served from 12.00pm-4.00pm and dinner is usually served around 8.00pm and on the weekends even later.

Business Hours

Business hours in Reykjavik differ depending on the season. In winter time many businesses are open from 09.00am to 5.00pm, and during the summer months of June, July and August they will close at 4.00pm.

Shopping centers and stores are usually open from 09.00am to 6.00pm on the weekdays. On Saturdays, opening times will be the same - 10.00am, but closing times can vary from 1.00 pm to 2.00 pm to 4.00pm. Shops and stores are generally closed on Sundays, but some supermarkets will be open until 11.00pm every day of the week.

Banks are open from Monday to Friday 09.15am-4.00pm.

Key Closure Days

During the winter season, there are a few days when businessesclose much earlier than usual.

On the day before Christmas, for example, most businesses will either not be open, or will close at noon.

Businesses also close early on December 31st and on January 1st.

The Thursday and Friday before Easter and Easter Monday are official holidays in Iceland and everything is closed.

Labor Day is celebrated for three days on the first weekend of August as an official holiday and everything is closed on that Monday.

11 ADDITIONAL REYKJAVIK ATTRACTIONS

Reykjavik offers a wide variety of attractions that can satisfy anyone's taste. Here are the city's *other* main highlights, which you definitely should try to include in your itinerary.

Runtur is a bar crawl that takes places on the weekends. It starts after midnight and it guarantees you a lot of fun. It takes place in Laugavegur and last until early morning hours. (There is also a Runtur on March 1, which celebrates the end of the Icelandic prohibition on beer.)

Pearl is a dome shaped building made of glass that features a revolving restaurant, the Saga Museum (dioramas illustrating some of the more popular scenes from the famous Icelandic Sagas) and an observation platform on the 4th floor. It is located on the Öskjuhlíd Hill. *Opening hours are every day from 10.00am-10.00pm. The restaurant is open till 11.00pm* http://perlan.is/

Vidistadatun Sculpture Park is situated in the middle of a lava field, located in the neighborhood of Hafnarfjordur (the "town in the lava.") In addition to a playground and a pond visitors can wander around looking at the 16 larger-than-life-size sculptures that were created as a part of the art festivals in 1991 and 1993, such as a gigantic art deco rotary phone and an ornate dragon.

http://www.visithafnarfjordur.is/art-and-culture/sculpture-park/

Imagine Peace Tower is a memorial to the singer John Lennon; a beautiful wishing well-shaped construction with colorful lights up in the sky. Located on Videy Island, it is only lit up on certain days of the year, such as the birthdays of John Lennon or that of his wife, Yoko Ono.

http://imaginepeacetower.com/

Grotta Lighthouse is located in a peaceful neighborhood of Seltjarnarnes. As the name implies, it's the perfect place to view the Northern Lights when they are in season. Bird lovers also congregate here.

Reykjavik Art Museum has its collection in three different buildings in the city; in Tryggvagötu, Sigtún and Flókagata streets. Each of them have different collections from statues, painting and other art works.

http://www.listasafnreykjavikur.is/

Strokkur is a magnificent geyser that blows hot water about 100 feet into the air. You can catch it on camera as it blows water approximately every 7 minutes. It is located in Haukadalsvegur.

Whale watching is a popular activity here. You will have a chance to see whales and a few more animal species in their natural habitat.

Hofsstadir Historic Park is located in Kirkjulundur, about 9 km from the city center. It showcases the excavations of a Viking-age longhouse (so large that it is estimated to have been the living area for over 20 individuals) and the whole area dates from that period. You can visit daily and the admission is free.

http://www.nat.is/hofstadir_gardabaer.htm

Bridge Between Continents, located several km southwest of Reykjavik on the Reykjanes Peninsula. There's a footbridge here (Leif the Lucky's bridge) spanning a rift in the Mid Atlantic Ridge that is a symbolic connection between Europe and North America.

12 ICELANDIC LANGUAGE ESSENTIALS

When you are traveling to a foreign country, it is good and useful to know some of the most frequent phrases in their language. They will come in handy for everyday situations, like greetings, looking for directions or when you arrive at the hotel. Here are some of the phrases in Icelandic with pronunciation that you should learn when going to Reykjavik.

Greetings:

Hello

Halló

(*Hah-low*)

Goodbye

Bless

(*Bless*)

Good morning

Góðan dag

(*Go-den-dog*)

Good evening

Gott kvöld

(*Got kvur-lt*)

Good night

Góða nótt

(*Goh-dha no-ht*)

Social:

Thank you very much.

Takk fyrir

(*Tak firir*)

No, thank you

Nei takk.

(*Ney tak*)

Please

Vinsamlegast (*Vin-sam-le-gast*)

Excuse me

Fyrirgefðu (*Firir-gef-du*)

How are you?

Hvernig hefur þú það?

(*Hver-nig hefur thu-thad*)

What's your name?

Hvað heitir þú?

(*Hvad hei-tir thu?*)

My name is...

Ég heiti...

(Ye-*heyti...*)

Where are you from?

Hvaðan ertu?

(*Hva-dan ertu?*)

Directions:

How do I get to _____?

Hvernig kemst ég til _____?

(Kver-nik kem-st ye til _____?)

Where is _____?

Hvar er _____?

(Kvar er _____?)

...the bus stop?

...strætóstopp?

(...strigh-toh-sto-hp?)

...the bus station?

...strætóstöðin?

(...strigh-toh-stur-dhin?)

...the coach station?

...biðstöðin?

(...bidh-stur-dhin?)

...the airport?

...flugvöllurinn?

(...*blu-kvojt-lur-inn?*)

...downtown?

...niður í miðbæ?

(*ni-dur ee midh-bye*) "*bye*" like English "Bye"

...the youth hostel?

...farfuglaheimilið?

(...*far-fuk-la-hay-mil-idh?*)

...the guest house?

...gistihúsið?

(...*gi-sti-hoos-idh?*)

Where are there ...

Hvar eru ...

(*Kvar eruh...*)

...a lot of hotels?

...mörg hótel?

(...*muhrg hoh-tel?*)

...a lot of restaurants?

...mörg veitingahús?

(*...muhrg vay-tin-ka-hoos?*)

...a lot of bars?

...margar krár?

(*mar-gawr krowr*)

...a lot of sites to see?

...margir ferðamannastaðir?

(*...mahr-gihr fer-dha-man-na-sta-dhir?*)

Can you show me on the map?

Gætiru sýnt mér á kortinu?

(*Gai-tiru see-nt m-yer a kort-inu?*)

street

stræti

(*strigh-ti*)

turn left

fara til vinstri

(*fa-ra til vin-stri*)

turn right

fara til hægri

(*fa-ra til high-kri*)

left

vinstri

(*vin-stri*)

right

hægri

(*high-kri*)

straight ahead

beint áfram

(*bay-nt aw-fram*)

north

norður

(*nor-dhur*)

south

suður

(*su-dhur*)

east

austur

(*ur-ee-stur*)

west

vestur

(*ve-stur*)

At the Restaurant:

I am hungry

Èg er svangur.(male)

(*Ye-er shvan-gur*)

Èg er swöng. (female)

(*Ye-er shvung*)

I would like to order.

Èg er tilbúinn að panta.

(*Ye-er-tilbooin ad panta*)

May I have the bill, please?

Gæti ég fengið reikninginn?

(Gigh-ti ye fen-kidh-rehnigen)

Waiter

þjón

(thyon)

The food and service were excellent.

Maturinn og þjónustan var frábær.

(Maturin-*oh thyonu-stan var frow-ber*)

At the Hotel:

Do you have any rooms available?

Áttu laus herbergi?

(*Ow-tu luhys her-ber-ki?*)

I'd like a single/double room

Gæti ég fengið einsmanns herbergi/tveggjamanna herbergi.

(*Gigh-ti ye fen-kidh ay-ns-mans her-ber-ki/tvek-ja-ma-na her-ber-ki.*)

Does the room come with...

Kemur það með...

(Ke-mur thadh medh...)

...bedsheets?

...rúmfötum?

(...room-furt-ohm?)

...a bathroom?

...klósetti?

(...kloh-se-htee?)

...a telephone?

...síma?

(...see-mah?)

...a TV?

...sjónvarp?

(...syohn-varpee?)

...a bath/shower?

...baði/sturtu?

(...ba-dhi/stuhr-tu?)

May I see the room first?

Má ég sjá herbergið fyrst?

(Maw ye syaw her-berg-ith fi-rst?)

Do you have anything quieter?

Ertu nokkuð með rólegri herbergi?

(Er-tu no-chk-udh medh roh-leg-rih her-ber-ki?)

...bigger?

...stærra herbergi?

(...sty-rah her-ber-ki?)

...cleaner?

...hreinna herbergi?

(...hraydna her-ber-ki?)

...cheaper?

...ódýrara herbergi?

(...oh-deer-a-ra her-ber-ki)

CONCLUSION

From eccentric museums and historic sites to world-class restaurants and bustling nightclubs, a visit to the city of Reykjavik is a magnificent journey that will please all your sense in a myriad of ways.

As a tourist hub, it might not be as popular as its European neighbors like Paris and Barcelona, Budapest, London and Vienna. Nevertheless, it is a rising star that will soon become a force to be reckoned with, as far as European tourism is concerned. With its peculiar character and diverse mix of attractions, Reykjavik may soon become one of the world's most sought-after destinations.

As you can see, there are a lot of exciting things you can do within three days in this European haven. From sightseeing to spine-tingling outdoor trips, the city has an endless array of activities to offer its beloved visitors and guests. If you can't get enough of Reykjavik in three days, extend your stay, and make sure to visit the other attractions of this wonderful country.

Made in the USA
San Bernardino, CA
30 April 2016